# BOLDLY QUIET

# BOLDLY QUIET

## THE INTROVERT'S GUIDE TO DEVELOPING THE MINDSET OF A SUCCESSFUL LEADER

Lorraine A. McCamley, MSOD

JONES MEDIA PUBLISHING

# DEDICATION

This book is dedicated to my father, Arthur D. Groves, a brilliant, kind, gentle, funny, quiet man.

# CONTENTS

# ACKNOWLEDGMENTS

Sincere gratitude is due to the current and past faculty of the University of Pennsylvania's Organizational Dynamics program who challenged me to see the world through different eyes. I would also like to acknowledge the contribution of Don Clifton and the Gallup Organization, whose CliftonStrengths® assessment challenged me to view myself differently. And, above all, I thank my husband, Mike McCamley, and our son, Tyler, who lovingly supported me on this roller coaster of a writing journey!

# INTRODUCTION

"You are not the type of leader [your company] values." Esteem-crushing words. Ambition-crushing words. Soul-crushing words. Did I still have a job? I felt as if I had just been fired even though I had been handpicked to undergo this psychological evaluation to determine the future investment the company would make in my leadership development. How could it happen that I went from top performer to a marginalized leader with those few words from a third-party psychiatrist? How could I continue to face human resources leaders, my boss and his peers, knowing they had discussed how I fell short of the company's defined leadership competencies?

As I struggled to get my career moving in a positive direction again, I felt my talents and strengths were not good enough. The mindset of "I am an introverted woman so I can't be successful without pretending to be someone else" continued to color my thinking, behavior, and, ultimately, my results. This belief became my mantra when I walked in the building every day, knowing I had to fight to be perceived differently. I knew to be successful I needed to force myself to act like someone I inherently was not. I left at the end of each day discouraged and exhausted, feeling stuck and undervalued.

My story is not unique. When I tell people I coach introverted leaders, heads nod and I hear about the struggles of pretending to fit an extroverted stereotype in order to be considered successful in many organizations. I hear frustration and self-doubt in their stories. And sometimes I hear anger as introverted professionals say they were passed over for promotions even though they outperformed the winning candidates on all levels—except fitting the most common stereotype of a successful leader: extroverted, charismatic, and bigger-than-life.

## SETTING THE STAGE

Let's take a moment before getting into the primary content of the book and come to a common understanding of how I view certain key terms and how I use them in the book. These terms are: introvert, extrovert, highly sensitive person, and successful leader. I acknowledge there are many different viewpoints on these concepts from very reputable sources. I have gravitated toward what has most resonated with me, how I view myself, and my experience in the workplace. I am grateful to Jacquelyn Strickland, LPC, who spent time with me discussing the nuances between and among introvert, extrovert, and highly sensitive person, and who helped me by challenging my thinking on these terms.[1]

### *Introvert/Extrovert*

As soon as my infant son started to use his hands, I could tell he was going to be left-handed. His strong, natural inclination was to reach for and grab things with his left hand and only use his right hand if his left hand was not in a position to be used. My husband is also left-handed. Shortly before we were married, he broke his left hand in a car accident. As a result, he was forced to use his right hand for

4

several weeks. It felt awkward, took more time, and he struggled. His left hand eventually healed and he was able to go back to what came more naturally to him.

The Latin definitions of "introvert" and "extrovert" are to turn ("vert") inward ("intro") and outward ("extra"). As an introvert, my natural tendency is to turn inward as I navigate through life. There are times, however, when I am required to turn outward. I speak sometimes for various groups. I go to parties where I have a wonderful time. I go to networking events to build my business. In these contexts, I know I will be more successful "turning outward," even though it takes some effort and focus. But I am *not* pretending to be someone I'm not. I am being authentic in my desire to interact with the people in the room. I am just choosing to interact with these people in a way that is not my most natural inclination.

At times it is harder for me to interact with life by turning outward. For example, if I am under a great deal of stress or am overly tired, it is incredibly hard for me to turn outward. One of the services I offer through my business is coaching through change. Organizational changes can cause introverted leaders to literally shut themselves in their offices at the time when their followers need to see them and interact with them. My job is to help the introverted leaders authentically turn outward, because that is what these types of situations demand. Again, this isn't about having introverted leaders pretend to be something they are not. It is about providing your followers with the support they need during a stressful time.

But wait. What about introverts as "reflective, cerebral, bookish, unassuming, sensitive, thoughtful, serious, contemplative, subtle, introspective, inner-directed, gentle, calm, modest, solitude-seeking,

5

shy, risk-averse, thin-skinned?"[2] In her book, *Quiet: The Power of Introverts in a World That Can't Stop Talking,* Susan Cain deliberately makes her definition of introvert very broad. In the same vein, I am deliberately choosing to use a very simple definition of introvert because, even though others may perceive me according to some of the attributes that Susan Cain has listed, that is not how I see myself. When I look inside, I see boldness, bright colors, and power. Many people, however, can relate to at least some of the attributes in Cain's broader description. A subset of these people may actually fall into the "highly sensitive" category.

## Highly Sensitive People

For some of you, the term "highly sensitive" or its area of research, sensory processing sensitivity, may be new. The four characteristics associated with being highly sensitive, however, are probably familiar. Research psychologist Dr. Elaine Aron uses the acronym of D.O.E.S. to describe these four characteristics:

- Depth of Processing
- Over Stimulation
- Emotional Responsiveness & Empathy
- Sensitive to Subtleties

And, contrary to what many would assume, both introverts and extroverts can be highly sensitive.[3] Introducing the concept of highly sensitive into the dialogue helps clarify why many people who are on the quieter side don't feel they fit the broader stereotype of an introvert—or many people who generally consider themselves to be extroverts often need to retreat when overstimulated. This book is not focused on highly sensitive introverts and extroverts, but I wanted to take this opportunity to introduce readers to the concept and provide them with a resource to learn more.

## Successful Leader

A 2017 *Harvard Business Review* (HBR) article discusses the unrealistic, yet pervasive stereotype of the ideal CEO, which mirrors and is influenced by the CEOs of Fortune 500 companies:

> . . .a successful CEO is a charismatic six-foot-tall white man with a degree from a top university, who is a strategic visionary with a seemingly direct-to-the-top career path and the ability to make perfect decisions under pressure.[4]

In this book, I define successful leadership through the eyes of followers. Chapter 2 goes into more detail about the four things that followers look for in their leaders: trust, compassion, stability, and hope. The challenge, however, is many organizations consciously or unconsciously define a successful leader like the caricature noted in the HBR quote above. Leaders who are more introverted pretend to be something they are not in order to fit that stereotype. How is this different than the introverted leader authentically turning outward when needed? The authentic leader isn't trying to be something he or she is not. The authentic leader is strategically turning outward to achieve a specific, desired goal. The leader who is pretending to be something he or she is not is literally trying to become someone else.

For purposes of this book, however, I am simply focusing on people, no matter what they call themselves, who feel caught between the desire to be a successful leader and the perception within many organizations that successful leaders are—or at least act like—a caricature of an extrovert.

## A Distorted Mindset

Any type of label that is perceived as being negative can become a self-fulfilling prophecy as the person—in this case, an introvert—begins to believe the negative perceptions are true. Many introverts develop a distorted view of themselves as they hear these comments at home, school, and in the workplace:

"You're too quiet."
"You need to promote yourself."
"No one knows how you are contributing."
"You have to be more inspiring to your team."
"You need to speak up more in meetings."
"You're so quiet, I didn't even know you were there."
"You have to be more charismatic."

These types of comments, while often meaning well, can send this message to the introvert: "You're not good enough as you are . . . you need to become something different." And to an introvert, that "something different" is a goal that often represents exhausting effort with minimal success.

When I was studying for my master's degree and participating in group learning activities, many extroverts felt they needed to invite introverts to participate, saying things like, "Let's give the quiet ones a chance to talk now." I knew the extroverts leading the conversations meant well, but I found myself becoming angry. I didn't need to be given permission to speak. If I had something I felt was important to say, it was my responsibility as a member of the group to speak up. But in this age of inclusion, where people are rewarded just for participating, introverts run the risk of becoming used to relying on others to be visible or heard. Waiting for permission or an invitation from others will often lead to missed opportunities and misperceptions of the value that the introvert brings to a discussion.

These feelings of not being good enough as you are or of needing to be invited to participate can lead to ever-deepening self-doubt. Maybe your prior accomplishments were just flukes. Perhaps the extroverts are just smarter than you are. Maybe you don't really deserve to have the position you do. This pattern of feelings is called the "imposter syndrome," where you fear being exposed as a fraud. In her book *Presence*, Amy Cuddy describes imposter syndrome as "the deep and sometimes paralyzing belief we have been given something we didn't earn and don't deserve, and at some point we'll be exposed."[5]

This fear, which can permeate your mindset, is incredibly detrimental in today's business environment, where the pace is fast, interactions are complex, and teamwork and collaboration are critical. Picture a star baseball player experiencing a hitting slump. The longer the slump lasts, the more worried the player becomes, adding to an already negative mindset that then perpetuates the poor performance. The same is true of a self-doubting mindset in a business environment. You will begin to shy away from opportunities and relationships which will reinforce your feelings of being a fraud and impact your performance as a leader.

A psychologist in the Philadelphia area, Cindy Schwartz-DeVol, Ph.D., recently told me this story about Marie (not her real name), a client of hers:

*When Marie began to see me, she was 33, recently promoted to supervisor at her job, and feeling quite insecure in her role, especially dealing with a difficult supervisee. Due to a history of being highly sensitive, introverted, and bullied as a child, those old insecurities were easily triggered. We worked on differentiating between old messages she learned and internalized and what her healthy adult self could tell her about her abilities and intuition. Marie learned how to reframe negative thoughts to more helpful and appreciative ones, that over time and with repetition, helped her build a healthier self-concept.[6]*

Have you ever had an eye exam? The phoropter is the instrument you look through while the optometrist asks, "Which is better, the first or the second?" Sometimes the phoropter's settings are such that you can't even identify any of the letters on the eye chart. But when the settings match your needed prescription, the eye chart is crystal clear. When we, as introverts, allow self-doubt to drive how we view ourselves and our ability to perform well as leaders, we essentially have the wrong prescription in our glasses and will not be able to accurately assess ourselves or the situations we are in because of the distortion.

## SHIFTING YOUR MINDSET

What if you put on a different pair of glasses, ones that allow you to not only clearly see, but also celebrate the unique blend of personality, passions, talents, skills, and experiences you offer as a leader? What if your feelings of frustration were replaced with feelings of freedom because you no longer had to pretend to be someone else? What if you knew how to position yourself to be respected as a successful leader within the context of your organization?

The purpose of this book is to provide you, the reader, with a new pair of glasses that will change how you look at yourself as a person and as a leader. This fresh, clear, perspective—or mindset—is presented to you in the form of *The Boldly Quiet Manifesto,* my declaration to myself as I sought to change how I viewed myself so I could adjust the perceptions of others. I am proud to share my manifesto with you.

# 1

# THE BOLDLY QUIET MANIFESTO

A manifesto is a declaration describing to others—and perhaps yourself—your intentions. The purpose for the American colonists' *Declaration of Independence* was to formally state the colonists' intentions of breaking free from the British crown. Martin Luther King's *I Have a Dream* speech inspired many during the U.S. Civil Rights movement. John F. Kennedy's *Land a Man on the Moon* speech focused the nation on space travel, culminating in Neil Armstrong's moonwalk in 1969. Manifestos are inspiring, future-focused, and sometimes controversial. They represent a new mindset or mission that will alter thinking, behavior, and, ultimately, results. Manifestos paint a vivid picture of a new ideal state—an independent country, freedom from racial injustice, winning the space race—and unite people to work toward accomplishing that goal. At their core, however, manifestos are an attempt to solve a problem where the current state of affairs is not acceptable and the desired future state is better.

## STARTING A NEW BUSINESS

Over the ten years that followed being told I wasn't the type of leader my company valued, I received a master's degree in organizational dynamics from the University of Pennsylvania, was subject to two job eliminations, became a Gallup-Certified Strengths Coach, and launched my own coaching and consulting business. Even as I was convinced starting my own business was the right next step for me, I struggled with self-doubt. Did I have what it takes to thrive as an entrepreneur? Would I be able to build my client pipeline so I could experience financial success? I thought back to something I had learned during my master's program: Russell Ackoff's four ways of dealing with problems:

1. *Absolution:* ignore the problem and hope it goes away without any action on your part;
2. *Resolution:* do enough to make the problem not as painful;
3. *Solution:* do something that yields the best possible outcome based on current state; and
4. *Dissolution:* redesign the situation so the problem disappears.[7]

As I sat in my home office those first few days, I ignored the problem of my self-doubting mindset. I made myself really busy. I set up my computer, found cool software and apps to help my business run smoothly, and I printed out a lot of articles I thought would make me a better consultant. I connected with as many people on LinkedIn as I could and let my friends and former colleagues know I had started my own business. And nothing changed.

Then I thought, I will make my problem of self-doubt less painful by signing up for every networking event I can. I will meet people and collect business cards and everyone will want to hire me because, after all, I have a great mix of business experience, academic depth, and personal strengths (at least, according to Gallup). So I wore myself out, afraid to miss any event because that might be the one where I would meet my first big client. And I dutifully went through the collected business cards the next day, inviting people to connect on LinkedIn, following up with emails about opportunities where they could engage my services for their companies. And very little changed.

I finally decided I needed a coach myself. I was very busy, but obviously not doing the right things to be successful. Perhaps having a coach would be the right solution. I signed up for a virtual mastermind class taught by Jo Self, a Strengths Branding coach[8], so I could solve my problem of conquering my self-doubt through attaining business. Jo asked me, "Who were you ten years ago? Start there when defining your target market." Ten years ago I was an introverted business leader struggling to be successful in an environment that favored extroverts. Great! I will become "The Introvert's Executive Coach." And more started to change. People were intrigued when I told them I focused on coaching introverts. After a speaking engagement, people would wait to talk to me and share their stories about the struggles of being an introvert. People began to follow me on LinkedIn because the content I shared was relevant and challenging. But I still carried my self-doubting mindset.

## Dissolving the Old Mindset

When my coach, Jo, and I began to discuss the redesign of my business brand, she asked me to write down key points about myself and my business I wanted to incorporate into my brand. Who am I? What are my strengths? What do I bring to the table and how do I deliver it? I spent a great deal of time reflecting on my past, both my failures and successes. I thought about what it was like to be an introvert as a child, as a student in a classroom, and as a business professional. I remembered the frustration of missing opportunities to speak in meetings because I didn't have time to think through what I wanted to say before speaking. I re-experienced the anger of feeling I couldn't escape from people's often incorrect perceptions of me. I began to think things like:

"I don't want to be safe."
"I don't need permission to speak up."
"I like bright colors and energetic words."
"I like to say funny things and laugh out loud."
"I don't want others to define me—I want to define me."
"I want to be responsible for my own success."

Quite frankly, I began to develop quite an attitude. Coupled with the recent advent of the *#MeToo* movement, I actually became a bit aggressive in certain contexts, with "I am proud to be an introverted woman" coloring my thoughts and words. Now, perhaps I was on the type of disruptive path I needed to take to dissolve my self-doubting mindset and replace it with a new, forward-looking frame of mind.

I began to make my list for Jo, trying to communicate to her the attitude I wanted to see incorporated into my new brand. The first bullet point on my list was easy:

### I WILL EMBRACE WHO I AM

I was tired of pretending to be someone else. I was tired of wishing I was different. I wanted to get to a point where I could recognize and celebrate my uniqueness—without apology. I wanted to accept myself with compassion. I wanted to laugh at myself when I made a mistake. I wanted my brand to say, "I am OK with myself, and I can help you be OK with yourself as well."

The second bullet point followed relatively easily, but flies a bit in the face of conventional thoughts about introverts:

### I WILL EMBRACE OTHERS

If one of my goals was to become a successful leader, how could I do that without "others"—direct reports, peers and colleagues, senior leaders, board members, vendors, and so on. Maybe I would need to figure out a different way to connect with others, a more authentic way, where I was not pretending to be an extrovert. My brand needed to be outward-facing, inviting others in, not just internally focused.

The third bullet point in my list addressed an area of huge frustration for me . . . missing opportunities to promote myself and my team in meetings:

17

## *I* WILL BE HEARD

I realized how tired I was of feeling that I failed to present my thoughts and opinions in meetings, or even in discussions around the water cooler. The self-dialogue of "I should have said this" or "I should have said that" haunted me as I walked back to my office. What if I prepared differently? And, instead of waiting for others to give me permission to speak, what if I had given myself permission to speak sooner, before my thoughts were fully formulated?

The next item on my list for Jo came about because I wanted others to see the boldness lurking inside of me:

## *I* WILL BE VISIBLE

I love the fact that, without saying a word, I can portray an authentic, confident leader who does not hide in the shadows, but instead draws attention to herself by making eye contact, sitting in the front of a room, and wearing bright colors. If I make it a point to be the first to welcome others into a room or seek out others standing by themselves to make them feel comfortable, I will be seen and I will be remembered.

The next bullet point is about taking care of myself:

## *I* WILL BREATHE

I need room to breathe, especially after an extended period of high stimulation. How many hours in a row can I have back-to-back meetings and stay sharp and engaged? What if I scheduled short breaks to take a brief walk? What if I took a moment before each meeting to take five deep, cleansing breaths? Would I sit up taller in my chair? Would I feel more confident? I think I would.

The next item I put on my list for Jo is a reminder to me of how fun it can be to disrupt other people's perceptions of me:

### I WILL SURPRISE

Stop making assumptions about me! You don't really know me! To emphasize that, I will periodically do the unexpected to make you look twice, and perhaps make the box you have built around me a little bit bigger. I will enjoy giving you a glimpse inside so perhaps you will see I am more than the caricature of an introvert.

I thought I was done with my list at this point, until I found myself putting together a proposal to lead a week-long women's leadership development workshop in North Macedonia. Then I realized I needed one final bullet point:

### I WILL GROW

Not only do I want to periodically challenge other people's perceptions of me by doing the unexpected, I want to continually challenge my own perception of myself. "I will grow" is about pushing myself to be more than I am today, about surrounding myself with the brightest and best, about embracing and learning from failure, about getting a little closer to the edge with my eyes open and my heart racing.

## CREATING THE NEW MINDSET

As I reviewed and refined my seven-item list, I felt the power and inspiration behind the words. My first thought was, "Wow, I wish I was like this." My second thought was, "I can be like this." My third thought was, "I can help others get there as well." Thus was born *The Boldly Quiet Manifesto*, the mental blueprint for authentically excelling as an introverted business leader, and the outline for the rest of this book.

# 2

# I Will Embrace Who I Am

*I don't have to be ashamed I am wired differently from more stereotypical leaders. I am unique and bring talents, skills, and perspectives to the table that are valuable and worthy of consideration. I cheapen my value to myself and others when I pretend to be someone else.*

What leader has had the most positive influence in your daily life? What three words best describe what this person contributes to your life? Gallup asked these questions to a random sampling of 10,000 people in a formal study from 2005–2008, which Tom Rath and Barry Conchie discuss in their book, *Strengths Based Leadership*[9]. These open-ended questions allowed the responders to describe leadership in their own words without being biased by categories such as "visionary" or "character." Gallup then studied the 25 most commonly mentioned words and was surprised words that many of us would expect—purpose, wisdom, humor, and humility—were not at the top of the list. The four basic needs of followers, identified through this study, are: *trust, compassion, stability*, and *hope*. My question for you is, when you look at yourself in the mirror, do you trust yourself? Do you treat yourself with compassion? Do you provide stability today and hope for tomorrow?

Replace my name with your own as you read this paragraph:

> When I look at Lorraine, I see someone who is incredibly trustworthy—she is authentic, competent, and looks out for my best interests—and she doesn't turn away from me or speak down to me when I fail or am struggling with a problem at work or in my personal life. Lorraine's character is strong and consistent, so I feel secure with her, and she gives me hope by always working toward a better future.

Those words sound odd when you say them about yourself, but if you are or aspire to be a successful leader, that is what others will say about you. Is your mindset such that you believe what is being said because you embrace who you are?

Let's look at each of the four basic needs of followers in a way that allows you to see yourself as you hope others see you. In the following sections, I focus primarily on the concept of trusting yourself and just touch on compassion, stability, and hope, because I believe learning to trust yourself is foundational—and perhaps the most challenging of the four.

## Trust

Many factors influence trust. When I speak about trust in complex business environments, I focus on competence (can you do what I need you to do?), benevolence (are you looking out for me?), consistency (can I predict how you will act?), risk (in this situation, what is the downside for me?), and alignment (do you share my values or goals?). In this context of trusting yourself, however, I will focus on *authenticity* and *competence*.

*Authenticity* is having a clear and complete picture of who I am and not pretending to be somebody else. I am reminded of an ancient fable of the elephant and three blind men. The blind men were positioned in different places around the elephant. One of the men felt the elephant's leg and thought the elephant was a tree. Another man felt the elephant's ear and thought the elephant was a fan. The third man felt the elephant's tusk and thought the elephant was a spear. Since the blind men could not see the entire elephant, their perception of the elephant was limited to only what they could feel in front of them.

Like the blind men, many of us have a limited idea of who we are, focusing on the most visible characteristics, often dwelling on the more negative aspects of those characteristics. One commonly used visual model of our literal blind spots is the Johari Window, created by Joseph Luft and Harry Ingham[10]. The 2 x 2 chart (Figure 1) has the following quadrants:

1. What I know about myself that others also see (open areas)
2. What I know about myself that others don't see (hidden areas)
3. What I don't know about myself that others see (blind areas)
4. What I don't know about myself that others don't see (unknown areas)

Figure 1: Johari Window

| | Known by self | Unknown by self |
|---|---|---|
| Known by others | Open areas | Blind areas |
| Unknown by others | Hidden areas | Unknown areas |

The goal of the Johari Window exercise is to expand your open areas and minimize your blind and hidden areas so you—and others— see your authentic self and no surprises emerge in the form of unconscious biases (from the blind areas) or deceptive behaviors (from the hidden areas). My preferred method of helping business leaders get a clearer picture of their authentic selves is through 360° assessments and individual coaching.

A 360° assessment is designed to gather feedback from your boss, peers, direct reports, and other constituents such as board members, internal and external customers, and business partners. Some 360° assessments also include friends and family members to provide an even broader set of feedback. Those completing the assessment generally provide their feedback anonymously (except, of course, your boss) and the assessment is usually completed in the form of an online survey. I have seen more positive results, measured by the level of acceptance from the participant and the usefulness of the data collected, from the interview method of collecting 360° feedback. While this may be cost prohibitive in some instances, the benefits are many:

- The coach can obtain context around responses and so provide more robust feedback.

- The coach can eliminate the noise in the feedback and focus on key themes around strengths and derailers.
- The person being assessed won't be sidetracked by random outliers or answers to questions that don't fit the reason the assessment is being given.
- The coach can frame the feedback in a way that will be most accepted by the person being assessed.
- Since the people being interviewed essentially practice their feedback when they give it to the coach, the people being interviewed may then feel comfortable giving their feedback directly to the person being assessed.

While undergoing a 360° assessment can seem intimidating, the themes that emerge from the interviews provide you with a clear picture of your blind areas and confirm your open areas. And an effective coach can help you take the feedback and create a development plan to address the feedback in an appropriate, affirming way.

The concept of *competence* is both in the present and forward-looking: Am I confident I can successfully accomplish what I need to do today? And am I confident I can do the things I may be called upon to do tomorrow? While you can look at your actual achievements to determine your competence at what you are being asked to do today, you must know your strengths in order to judge whether you have the capacity to be successful tomorrow.

## The CliftonStrengths® Assessment

Don Clifton, the mind behind the CliftonStrengths® assessment (formerly StrengthsFinder®), asked the question, "What would happen if we studied what was right with people versus what's wrong with people?"[11] Psychology to that point had followed the same track as the study of medicine, focusing on pathology, not wellness. In the late 1990s, Clifton and a team of scientists looked for patterns in over 100,000 talent-based interviews of people who were considered successful. The ultimate result was a common language of Strengths, with 34 themes, and an assessment that identifies a person's level of intensity in each of those themes.

In *Soar with Your Strengths*, Clifton and his co-author, Paula Nelson, describe a myth borne from the power of positive thinking school of thought: "Everyone can do anything they put their minds to." Does that mean if I work hard and think the right thoughts I will be successful? I don't think so. When I was in high school I had two primary extracurricular activities: piano lessons and competitive swimming. I was naturally talented in music, so progressed on the piano well beyond my peers with probably less effort. I was not so talented in swimming, but I really wanted to excel as a swimmer. No matter how hard I tried, however, I was mediocre at best.

I took the CliftonStrengths® assessment in 2010 through my organization, and it was the first time I remember seeing certain aspects of myself through a positive lens. I had always been a solid performer based on my work output, but there were always caveats that started with, "but you need to be more (*fill in the blank*)." All of a sudden, I had a list of my top ten or so Strengths I could develop and strategically draw on in order to excel at my job. Sure, I tend to be quiet . . . but I am mentally busy using my Analytical (#4) and Intellection (#5) Strengths. And, yes, I struggle with forced group social activities . . . but I love to use my Responsibility (#1) and Relator (#2) Strengths, where I advocate for my team, organization, and clients. I began to learn focusing on what was right with me (i.e., my strengths) and then using my strengths to manage my weaknesses was a more authentic route to becoming a successful leader. I have always struggled to speak when I am put on the spot. But now I know to prepare differently for interactions with others, analyzing agendas, trying to think through what ancillary topics may come up so I will have a head start crafting my "off the cuff" comments so I can speak with confidence.

Being explicitly aware of your strengths provides you with confidence that you have the means by which you can accomplish what you need to in the future. Knowing your strengths also allows you to appreciate that you are more than just an introvert. You think, behave, and are motivated differently than the introvert in the office next to yours. When you invest in developing your strengths, you unleash your unique potential in an authentic and highly competent way.

## COMPASSION

Followers also look for compassion from their leaders. Compassion is often confused with feelings of pity, sympathy, and empathy. To illustrate the difference, let's look at several people's hypothetical responses to a natural disaster 300 miles away where many homes were lost:

Amy: "Those poor people . . . why do they keep living in an area prone to disaster?"

Brad: "I hope things get better for the people who lost their homes."

Cathy: "I found myself crying when I watched the people who lost their homes on the news."

David: "I cried for the people who lost their homes and signed up to donate my vacation time to help them rebuild."

Amy looked on the people who lost their homes with pity, acknowledging their loss, but almost in a condescending way, like it was their fault. Brad also acknowledged the people's loss in a sympathetic, but non-engaged way. Cathy empathized with the people who lost their homes, feeling their feelings. David was the most engaged of the four, not only feeling the pain of the people who lost their homes, but also doing something to improve their situation. David was the one who had true compassion on the people who lost their homes.

How does this transfer to having compassion on ourselves? I tend to waiver between self-pity and self-compassion. "I feel awful I screwed up that presentation, but, of course I did, I can't do anything right" is the self-pity approach. How much better off would we be if we treated ourselves with compassion: "I feel awful I screwed up that presentation. I should ask my boss for some training in delivering presentations." Pity wallows, compassion moves forward. We have compassion on ourselves by not only admitting the pain, but also taking steps to do something positive about it.

## STABILITY

Another attribute that followers look for in their leaders is stability. Leaders who provide stability to their followers live according to well-defined values. They consistently follow their values and have the inner strength to stand up for what they believe. Can you articulate your values? In their book, *The Leadership Challenge: How to Make Extraordinary Things Happen in Organizations,* James Kouzes and Barry Posner discuss how important it is for leaders to clarify their values:

> The very first step on the journey to credible leadership is clarifying your values—discovering those fundamental beliefs that will guide your decisions and actions along the path to success and significance. That involves an exploration of the inner territory where your true voice resides. It's essential that you take yourself on this journey because it's the only route to authenticity . . . You can't do what you say if you can't say what you believe. And you can't do what you say if you don't believe in what you're saying.[12]

If you are not able to articulate your values, here are several questions you can ask yourself:

- What are the most important things in my life?
- What do I want people to say about me when I am not in the room?

29

- What are my non-negotiables when I try to solve a problem?
- What do I protect about myself or others?
- How do I spend my free time?
- How do I spend my money?

Once you have answered each of these questions, look for common themes, such as: honesty, equality, service, truth, success, and humor. This list of common themes will be at least a rough draft of your values. Continue to refine your values as you examine decisions you have made in the past and those you are being called on to make now. Then continue to build your foundation of inner strength and stability by consciously looking for how you can consistently apply your values in the future. Learn to appreciate your values as you see the positive impact they have on those around you. And trust yourself that decisions you make will be aligned with your values.

## HOPE

Followers want their leaders to inspire hope in the future. "Somewhere over the Rainbow," the Academy Award winning song from the movie *Wizard of Oz* (1939), paints a beautiful picture of hope. Picture a young Judy Garland, filmed in black and white, sitting with her dog, Toto, looking out into the distance, singing words about a land where dreams come true that can be found beyond the rainbow. The character, Dorothy, knows there is more to her life than where she is today: a world filled with color where she can leave behind the troubles of her current situation and attain a new state of being that she can't picture, but knows it will be closer to her dreams.

What are your dreams? Intentionally identifying your dreams, even writing them down, will help you be more aware of opportunities around you that could actually be steps toward realizing your dreams. If one of your dreams is to be a Fortune 500 CEO one day, you can then set goals to work toward those dreams. Perhaps defining your dreams will help you take more risks in your career, asking a senior leader to mentor you, or pursuing stretch assignments. Perhaps articulating your dreams will help you look at yourself differently: someone living in a vibrant, technicolor world, not someone living in a state of black-and-white hopelessness.

## EMBRACING WHO YOU ARE

How would your mindset as a leader change if you could say this to yourself?

> *I trust myself. I know and value who I am, and look forward to learning even more about myself. I have unique strengths, skills, and experiences that make me good at what I do today and give me the capability to learn what I need to be good at tomorrow. I know I'm not perfect, and I do not expect myself to be perfect. When I fail, which I will, I look at my failure as an opportunity to grow, not as a reason to continually berate myself. I know what my values are and consistently use them as a beacon to direct my path, both short-term and long-term. I allow myself to hope in a future where I am far beyond where I am today, and I identify and diligently pursue opportunities to make that future a reality.*

If you could say this to yourself, figuratively embracing yourself, how do you think it would change how you react to others, whether or not you are an introvert?

*I will embrace who I am.*

# 3

# I Will Embrace Others

*While my energy may come from within, my sense of purpose as a leader is built upon equipping others to be successful. I will draw others out by asking insightful questions and really listening to their responses, helping them draw connections and conclusions that spur their personal and professional growth.*

Imagine sitting at your desk in your office, cubicle, or open environment. Your task list is long: you have things to do and things to think about. When I worked in the corporate world, I used to have a note taped to my telephone that said, "Walk and talk." I deliberately took the long route to the restroom just so I would walk by more people. My natural tendency was to focus on the work I needed to get done, taking minimal breaks, being responsive to emails, and attending meetings. I wasn't opposed to initiating friendly interaction with people. More often than not, I enjoyed engaging with others in the office. It just wasn't top of mind.

Who are the "others" in your workplace? Certainly, your boss and the people who report to you. What about other senior executives or board members, peers, customers, service providers, or vendors?

What mindset do you need to develop as a successful leader to embrace each category of constituents? Your mindset should include a desire to understand other people's perspectives, to help others be successful, and to equip others to help you be successful.

## Understanding Perspectives

At one point in my career, I served as the business' executive sponsor for a multi-million-dollar IT project. Our division's IT business partner was a great guy, but we consistently experienced conflict during our periodic status meetings when we discussed the project's budget projections. We would have the same conversation every time:

Me: We can't afford this change.

IT: We can request more project spend from the enterprise project pool.

Me: That doesn't matter. We still can't afford it.

IT: I know I can get it approved.

Me: That doesn't matter. Even if we can get the money, we still can't afford it.

And then we would both leave the discussion frustrated.

Then one day, my IT business partner and I went to lunch. We talked about how IT views and tracks project money and we talked about how the business views and tracks project money and the differences in the two approaches. We left lunch committed to representing each other's perspectives back to our respectful organizations. We also left lunch with a stronger foundation of trust.

In his book *Shatter Your Leadership Limits: Better Results in Less Time with Less Stress*, Bob Kantor, an IT management consultant and executive coach, suggests we use negative feelings as a trigger to ask insightful questions:

> If we're in a meeting and someone is continually challenging us and we are finding ourselves getting more and more frustrated and angry, can we reframe our intent? What if our intent was no longer to argue with this person, but instead to truly understand why they see things so differently and are so passionate about that difference in perspective? . . . Would that change our emotional reaction? Would we cease being angry and frustrated? Would we, in fact, show up as curious, fully engaged, and interested in the other individual and what their thought process is?[13]

Intentionally seeking to understand other people's perspectives is an important component of the mindset of a successful leader. I recently had the honor of facilitating three Strengths workshops at the University of Delaware for a cohort of the 2019 Mandela Washington Fellowship program. The 25 fellows were young leaders representing countries in sub-Saharan Africa. During one of the exercises, the fellows had to react to various statements I made by physically positioning themselves based on the level they agreed (or disagreed) with my statement. One of my statements was something like, "I work just to pay bills; my work doesn't have to be fulfilling."

The majority of the class strongly disagreed with that statement. I asked one of the few fellows who were neutral on the statement why he felt the way he did, assuming he would say something about work ethic and downplaying the concept of employee engagement. His response illustrated for me the importance of taking the time to understand other people's perspectives: his country currently has an unemployment rate of 80%. In his country, the most important thing was having a job so you could feed your family. What a radically different reality than the one many of us will ever experience.

Will your team members share their perspectives with you? Or will your peers have an open conversation with you about their perspectives on a particular issue? This brings up the question of whether others feel psychologically safe with you. How will you react if you hear a perspective that is different from your own? Will you become combative? Will you listen with the intent of understanding without judgment? If you react negatively to what they are saying, will you assume their intentions are good and seek to better understand their perspective? Or will you proceed with a negative path that will ultimately harm your relationship? Will you discount their feelings by telling them they shouldn't feel that way? Or will you help them process those feelings so they can move forward?

Successful leaders embrace those they lead by setting clear expectations, giving them what they need to succeed, and promoting their team through recognition and stretch assignments. *In other words, successful leaders make those they lead successful by making sure they know how to shine, that they are able to shine, and that they have opportunities to shine.* Successful leaders must understand the perspectives and needs of their associates, and that requires authentic and frequent interactions.

Have you ever poured all your energy into a project only to find you did not understand your boss's expectations? That happened to me a few years ago, where I was left embarrassed and confused. How could I have missed the mark by so much? Was I not paying attention? Did I not ask the right questions? Setting clear expectations for your team members helps them prioritize their work, delegate when needed, and collaborate appropriately with others. Can you imagine running a race and not knowing where the finish line is? You won't know whether to sprint or pace yourself, or whether you are even on the right path.

Since I process most of my thinking internally, I often make the assumption people can read my mind and have been following along on my mental journey. I developed a practice of documenting expectations and reviewing them during one-on-one conversations with my direct reports to make sure we were aligned. What should be included in these discussions of expectations? Not only the ultimate goals that show up on many performance reviews, but also milestones, timing, look and feel of the anticipated output, and how you want to be notified of progress or issues.

If, like me, those interactions are not naturally top-of-mind, I recommend leaning on the structure provided by your calendar. Schedule recurring meetings with standing agenda items that prompt the right dialogue. Are the two of you (or you and the team) aligned on expectations? Does each person have what they need to successfully and effectively get their work done? Do I know each person on the team well enough to allocate work according to their strengths?

Similarly, creating structure to intentionally request and receive feedback from other stakeholders, such as customers and vendors, will provide a forum to not only solve problems before they escalate, but also foster innovation and build partnerships. When you take the time to really understand your customers' needs today, you can begin to anticipate and address the needs they will have tomorrow. When you take the time to solicit feedback from your vendors, you begin to transform the relationship from master-servant to partner-partner, which could lead to future opportunities for collaboration.

## *Helping Others be Successful*

Coaching, mentoring, sponsorship, and partnership are ways you can intentionally help others be successful. These can be very structured programs or they can be informal, situational interactions. When programs are more formal, coaching, mentoring, and sponsoring are generally between people at two levels of the organization or, in the case of coaching, sometimes with a third-party professional. Let's look at some of the nuances among the different ways you can help others be successful, by replaying a scenario between Joe, a leader of a team of analysts, and Fran, one of Joe's direct reports.

*Coaching: Fran, is interested in getting ahead within the organization. Joe asks Fran if she thinks there is anything holding her back from applying for a new position. Fran isn't sure she is totally qualified for the new position. Joe helps Fran identify some skills she could attain and encourages her to ask her colleagues for input about areas she should focus on to be considered for the target position. Once Fran has her list, Joe helps Fran create a development plan so she can prepare for this next opportunity. Joe frequently checks in with Fran to see the progress she is making on her development plan and asks about her successes and challenges.*

*Mentoring: Fran, is interested in getting ahead within the organization. Joe asks Fran if she thinks there is anything holding her back from applying for a new position. When Fran indicates she isn't sure how to define and execute on her career path given some of the challenges she is facing, both at work and in her personal life, Joe suggests she seek out a mentor, someone who has experienced similar challenges and can help her navigate these challenges. Joe provides her with the names of two senior leaders he thinks would be willing to enter into this developmental relationship with Fran. While Joe doesn't monitor Fran's relationship with her mentor, he notices Fran seems more confident and less stressed.*

*Sponsorship: Fran is interested in getting ahead within the organization. Joe asks Fran if she thinks there is anything holding her back from applying for a new position. Fran is concerned she doesn't know the right people to be considered for the role. Joe says he will actively sponsor her for roles she would like to pursue—he will set up a meeting with the hiring manager to talk about Fran's fit for the role and will do his best to make sure she gets an interview.*

Coaching is targeted toward identifying—either informally through self-reflection and discussion with others or formally through assessments or third party interviews—areas of growth. A coach helps the person create goals and a development plan to reach these goals. Mentoring is a much more personal relationship between someone who has "been there, done that" and a less-experienced person struggling along a similar path. There is no set process, as there often is in coaching, and the mentoring/mentee relationship often includes a personal component. Because of this, many organizations recommend a mentor be outside of the reporting relationship. Regardless, the scope of the mentor/mentee relationship is broader and more open-ended than a coaching relationship. Effective sponsors intentionally promote their "sponsees" to others, putting their own reputations on the line as they look for ways to bring new opportunities to the ones they sponsor.

Unlike coaching, mentoring, and sponsoring, partnership is agnostic to organizational levels and reporting relationships and tends to be more project-specific. Successful partnerships involve at least two parties who work together toward a common goal, support and promote each other's activities, and assume good intentions when there is conflict. The best partnerships are founded on trust and are often successful because of some level of diverse thinking or experience. Often, however, leaders are expected to partner with peers whom they don't trust, don't like, or don't respect. Succeeding in this type of partnership can be much more challenging and warrants an entirely separate book! That being said, here are three ways to model how a partnership optimally operates:

1. Ask a lot of questions to make sure you understand the other person's position, especially if you sense tension;
2. Give negative feedback professionally and directly to the person in question, rather than complaining to others; and
3. Don't forget to give positive feedback when it is deserved— and give it in a sincere manner.

## Allowing Others to Help You

I was sitting in my office one day and received a personal call on my cell phone with very distressing news about a close friend of mine. I immediately closed my office door and began to cry as I tried to figure out how I could deal with this tragedy and fulfill my obligations at work. One by one, my team members rallied around me to ask how they could help—what meetings they could cover, what work they could continue—so I could take care of what I needed to do. When I was out of the office, one colleague emailed me and asked how she could help. My response, trying to be funny, was I could really use my caffeine of choice, a diet soda. When I got back to my office, a can of soda was on my desk with a brief, but very touching note. I keep that can of soda near my desk in my home office to remind me of the importance of allowing others to help me.

Allowing yourself to be vulnerable helps people feel closer to you, which, in turn, helps them feel good about themselves. We often are concerned about burdening others or being embarrassed. Deep down, however, no matter our level in the organization or tenure or pay grade, we all are humans who need each other and need to feel needed.

## Embracing Others Authentically

The most important point about embracing others is to do so in an authentic way. Have you noticed the word "introvert" hasn't come up very much since the beginning of this chapter? Our ability—or desire—to embrace others as successful leaders has very little to do with being an introvert or an extrovert. Being able to embrace yourself, having confidence in who you are, and allowing your authentic self to be seen by others, is what helps you embrace those around you. You feel free to be who you are, care for others in your own unique way, and help others be successful.

*I will embrace others.*

# 4

# I Will Be Heard

*I will prioritize "pre-thinking" so I can speak early in a
meeting about a planned topic. I will give myself permission to talk before my thoughts are fully formulated. I will
not assume others who talk more than I do know more
than I do, and will professionally insert my own thoughts
and questions into the dialogue. I will not wait for others
to create a "safe space"; neither will I wait to be invited to
speak.*

I'm sitting in a leadership team meeting—about ten of us around
a table with a few more dialed in remotely. I haven't said much to
this point because it seemed others addressed the comments I was
internally processing. I notice a couple of my peers just repackage
comments others have said. I find this irritating and feel a flash of
pride that I don't waste people's time saying things already said. Our
boss launches a discussion about a more controversial topic, and the
dialogue in the room becomes more energetic with people starting
to interrupt each other and speak more loudly and quickly. I find
myself struggling to process the varying viewpoints quickly enough.
The topic isn't one I am an expert on, so I haven't spent a great deal
of time thinking about it. As I just start to get my arms around what

others have said and begin formulating a response, the meeting ends and people leave the room. And I realized I said very little in the meeting but feel as though my positions were well represented by others.

Not too long after that leadership team meeting, I find myself sitting in a leadership development class where we are talking about effective communication: verbal, non-verbal, being a good listener, and appreciating different communication styles. We break into small groups, and the person who usually talks the most in any meeting I've been in with her assumes the role of discussion leader. Since the content isn't particularly engaging to me—I have been through similar training many times—I am content to listen and observe. Right before our time is up, the de facto group leader says something like, "Let's let the quiet ones have a chance to talk." My response, after convincing myself punching her wasn't a good course of action, was that I would have said something if I had something to add to the conversation.

During the course of my leadership journey with this company, I had the opportunity to participate in several 360° assessments. I was surprised when more than one person commented that I needed to "show up better" at meetings. After talking with my boss and my coach about this, I realized that, while I was content my viewpoints were being expressed so did not feel the need to talk, others were wondering why I had been invited to the meeting since I had very little to say. In addition, waiting until after the meeting to fully process and express my perspective on a given issue was not helpful to the group.

When I tell people the name of my company, Boldly Quiet Consulting, they start telling me stories about their own experience as an introvert or experiences they have had with others. This concept of being heard is the most prevalent theme I hear. People are frustrated others receive credit for their ideas, that they didn't have a chance to prepare properly for meetings, and that others assume they don't have anything to say. Sure, it's great introverts tend to be good listeners, but sometimes we need to be heard. Here are some simple things you can do to accomplish this.

## Prepare

Nothing is more important to a leader who is an "internal thinker" than investing the time to be prepared. In *The Introverted Leader: Building on Your Quiet Strength*, Jennifer B. Kahnweiler says, "Preparation is the first step. It is the series of actions that plays to the introvert's 'sweet spot' by doing what comes naturally . . . Preparation gives you confidence to handle situations as they emerge."[14] Any article you read about running an effective meeting includes having an agenda. Schedule time during your day to prepare for meetings. Perhaps your first hour of the day is designated as your meeting prep time for upcoming meetings. If your meetings are not back-to-back, perhaps you schedule time before each meeting so your thoughts are fresh. Regardless, give yourself time to think, gather data, and write down either what you want to say or questions you want to ask.

## Talk Early

Before the meeting starts, engage with agenda topic owners if they are available. Simply saying, "I'm looking forward to the discussion

45

about your topic" shows the presenter/facilitator you will be engaged in the discussion. And, if you have had the opportunity to prepare some thoughtful—or thought-provoking—comments or questions, be one of the first to raise your hands before the tempo of the conversation makes it harder for you to break in. Talking early is a signal to others you are engaged and have something to say. That perception will carry through the meeting and establishes your right to be in the room.

## Let Others Take a Peek

One of the best pieces of advice I received from the coach helping me to work through the 360° feedback of others (mentioned above), is I needed to "lower the bar" of when I felt my thoughts were "ready for prime time," i.e., formulated enough I was comfortable expressing them. By waiting until I finished my mental processing, I missed opportunities to be heard. Saying things like, "I would like to think about this some more, but I am leaning toward . . . " or "My initial thoughts on this topic are . . . " or "I need some more time to process this . . . can we schedule a follow-up meeting before we make a decision?" help others see—and learn to value—the mental process you are going through to be an effective member of the team.

## Say Something Provocative

Since I am a bit of a rebel inside, my favorite thing to do before meetings is to pick a topic I have energy around and think of something provocative to say or that I can be more assertive than normal about. I remember one particular meeting where I was reviewing the agenda and meeting materials and saw a pretty glaring issue with the materials for an agenda item where I was being asked to vote. Before the meeting, I decided I needed to be assertive about the issue I saw, if for no other reason than to prove to others I took my responsibility to vote seriously. I challenged the proposal—and felt good doing it—and promptly got in trouble after the meeting because I came off as not trusting my colleague. This led to an interesting discussion on why I was being asked to vote on something if I was just supposed to rubber-stamp my approval without question, a point my boss understood. Could I have handled the situation differently with the person making the proposal? Yes, perhaps I should have spoken to my colleague before the meeting. That being said, preparing a provocative comment about an important topic shows you are engaged in the discussion and have a right to be in the room—and that you are not afraid of conflict.

## Ask Questions

A coaching and consulting colleague of mine, Jan Stefanski, owner of Janus Consulting, recently told me this story:

> Bill was a leader in a pharmaceutical company and on a team with scientists, researchers, and commercial participants. He was very accomplished in his field: thoughtful in his approach, speaking up when he saw an incorrect statement, a suggestion that could cause trouble, or was asked a direct question. Bill shared with me how meetings would progress and how he would participate. I could see how he could be viewed by others as being 'non-value-add' because in their view of what being a good team member meant was always to be very outwardly actively engaged, very often leading/directing discussions,

*sometimes being emotional, etc. You get the point, a difference in style. My suggestion to Bill was this. Be who you are. <u>Continue</u> to be thoughtful, attentive to the discussion at hand with one other wrinkle. <u>Overtly</u> enter into the discussion on a regular basis. What's that mean? Get a watch/phone that can vibrate every 10-15 minutes. If you have not spoken in the last 10-15 minutes, lean forward at the table, take off your glasses and interject into the conversation by paraphrasing what had been recently said. To the speaker or group, say something like, "Can I just see if I am understanding what is being said? [Paraphrase it] Do I have it correct? Thanks."[15]*

Bill didn't change. Because he intentionally inserted himself into the conversation, the perception was he had changed—he appeared more engaged and stopped being a silent participant. He became an active partner.

## *Raise Your Hand*

One of the hardest things for me to do is to break into a spirited conversation where there are no natural pauses in the dialogue and my head is turning back and forth as if I was watching a ping pong match. In more formal settings, the answer is simple: raise your hand enough to get the facilitator's attention. There's a chance the meeting facilitator will welcome this type of interruption because he or she has been trying to figure out how to regain control of the discussion.

In more informal settings, you can also use body language to make the interruption. Picture yourself at a networking reception where you are standing with a small group of people, feeling uncomfortable because you want to say something but don't know how to break into the conversation. Try taking a step (literally) toward the middle of the group of people. Disrupting the physical space inhabited by the group will help capture attention and create a brief break in the conversation without you having to say a word. Be ready with your comment, however, or else the moment will be lost.

Another way to break into informal conversations is to lean toward the person speaking and reach out to them as if you are going to touch their arm (depending on the person, perhaps you could). Again, this is a way to disrupt the spacial dynamics within the group, and people will unconsciously pause.

## Public Speaking

*"You're an introvert? How did you get up the nerve to just give that talk?"*

Fear of public speaking is not just an introvert thing, and surveys often show people are more afraid of speaking in public than they are of death, heights, or spiders. Public speaking is actually a great way to be heard, because people don't interrupt you! I enjoy taking the time to carefully craft a message I care about and want to share with others. I enjoy watching heads nod as I drive home a point that resonates. Am I afraid I will stumble over my words? Sure, and I usually have some awkward pauses as I try to re-enter the flow of my presentation. That being said, I find my passion for my topic gives me a platform where I am perceived as being authentic and approachable. Here are some tips if you are open to trying public speaking:

1. Pick a topic you are passionate and knowledgeable about.
2. Sign up for training or coaching on structuring and delivering a talk.
3. Get help with the actual presentation to make sure it looks professional and is engaging.
4. Use stories and metaphors to engage your listeners.
5. Try to engage with the listeners prior to your talk. I like to stand by the door and welcome people as they come in to try to build rapport before I have even started.
6. Practice! And don't worry, when you practice in your hotel room in front of a mirror, your talk will probably be horrible because you are focused on yourself. But practicing helps you get through the stumbles when it is for real.
7. Start small, preferably with people who know you and will give you positive and constructive feedback.
8. Focus on how your audience is engaged with what you are saying, not on what you are afraid they are thinking about you.

Because most people are so afraid of public speaking, you gain automatic credibility by putting yourself on a stage. People will pursue your opinion about topics not because they feel sorry for you since you are an introvert, but because they know you have something to say.

## The Bottom Line

The bottom line is that as a leader you have to figure out how to be heard. No one needs to give you a voice, no one needs to empower you to speak: you have a voice, and with the right mindset and some simple strategies you will be heard. Make sure you are prepared with something meaningful to say and figure out a way to say it.

*I will be heard.*

# 5

# I WILL BE VISIBLE

*In professional settings, I will wear splashes of bright color that will help me stand out in the sea of gray, navy, and black. I will arrive early, sit in front, and smile and make eye contact with others. I will be the first to reach out to newcomers and others standing by themselves.*

One of the myths about introverts is we don't like to draw attention to ourselves. I periodically search online for famous women introverts, and many performers like Christina Aguilera, Courteney Cox, and Emma Watson are cited. Do we really want to avoid the spotlight? In some instances, sure: if you can get me on the dance floor, there is no way I am going into the middle of the circle like the finale of the movie *Footloose*! But I certainly don't hide when given the opportunity to draw attention to myself in a positive way when I feel good about myself, my results, or the group or opportunity I am representing.

When my son was in elementary school, my biggest worry was he would be invisible. He and I are very similar, and I knew if he wasn't confident he wouldn't raise his hand in class. And I was afraid his teachers would allow him to be invisible since he wasn't a troublemaker, making the incorrect assumption that teachers only spend time with the kids who draw attention to themselves. His wonderful teachers helped him gain the confidence he needed to raise his hand. His great teachers helped him be visible in group projects and by encouraging him to try new activities. Sometimes, we, as business leaders, need a similar nudge. We are going to look at several opportunities for introverted business leaders to intentionally raise their visibility, along with some simple tips on how to do so while remaining genuine.

## Office Meetings

I sat in a room of 200+ business leaders several years ago in a large banquet room. Each table held eight to ten people, and everyone was in suits or comparable business attire. When I surveyed the room, I estimated approximately 40% of the meeting attendees were women. Two of us in the room, myself and another woman, had on bright jackets. Everyone else in the room had on gray, navy, or black. I actually went up to the other woman at one of the breaks and congratulated her on standing out!

Intentional color placement is a very simple, fun way to be visible in a crowd without saying a word. I actually had a color analysis done when I was in my 20s, and found out I am a "winter"—think bright jewel tones or pure white, black, and navy blue. I am naturally drawn to these colors, and they create the perception of health and energy when I wear them. I can draw attention to myself simply by wearing these colors, without saying a word. My consulting "uniform" is usually black or navy pants with a bright jacket, with either a black or complementary bright blouse. Nail polish, fun shoes, or other accessories are "visibility tools" as well. People can find me in the room and, if I am the only person wearing bright colors, their eyes will naturally be drawn to me. You will find that it works for you as well.

Other ways you can be visible during meetings: be physically engaged in the meeting. Sit up front. When participants look at the meeting's primary speaker or facilitator, they will see you. Make eye contact with each person speaking rather than taking notes or looking at materials. Smile. Smiling naturally draws people closer. And if it's not an appropriate time to smile, raise your eyebrows slightly. This action brightens your face even though you're not smiling, and it communicates you are following along and interested in what the speaker is saying.

## Around the Office

For many introverts, the three most important words you can take from this book are "walk the halls." Be visible around the office. Take the longest route to the bathroom. If you have an office with a door, keep the door open. Eat in the main cafeteria or deli during peak times. If you have a permanent office or cubicle, decorate it in ways that tell people a little about you. And, since many introverts are perceived as being unengaged or distant, make your office space welcoming, giving visitors an insight into who you are.

## Networking

My colleague, Erin Owen, is an executive career reinvention coach. She told me the story of her client who was not only quiet, but faced some cross-cultural challenges and struggled to network:

> When [my client] was seeking to make new connections to explore opportunities for a summer business internship during his MBA, I talked with him about the fact that most people love to tell their stories about their career journeys—where they started and how their careers evolved to where they are today. When he heard this, he was thrilled. He loved asking people questions and listening to learn more about them. This idea gave him a strategy to use in creating connection with others he did not know very well or perhaps did not even know at all.[16]

I had no concept of the value of networking until I started my own company and business development became my responsibility. Sure, I went to internal events that were offered, but I quickly realized when I became a consultant that my external network was nonexistent. Networking is one of my most important marketing activities, and I have had to learn to make it work for me in a way that is not only effective, but enjoyable. Here are some tips that have worked for me:

- Do your research before the meeting. If you have access to the meeting attendees, determine the people it is important for you to meet or talk to and make it your mission to do so.
- If there is a topic being presented at the meeting, have a few questions or comments ready to go.

- Arrive early so there aren't many people in the room; everybody feels awkward at the very beginning! And it won't be as overwhelming as walking into a room full of people.
- Appoint yourself the welcoming committee for others who are standing by themselves. Then you won't have to worry about breaking into a group conversation, and you will definitely make a friend with the other person who is in the same boat as you are.

## *Reporting*

Does your boss—or your board if you are *the* boss—know what you do every day? Do they check in with you frequently to make sure you are on track? Once you reach a certain level in the organization, your boss most likely expects you to proactively provide information about your team's progress and challenges. For some of us, however, promoting ourselves can be a struggle. We feel like our work should speak for itself. But your boss may not have a direct line of sight into your work. Your boss may be in a different location or may be constantly out of the office. I found that developing a template I could update every one-two weeks that tracked key performance metrics and an area for narrative or bullet points was a helpful tool in providing my boss with the desired information without making me feel I was bragging. This also gave my boss a quick-reference tool regarding my team and its progress.

## Volunteering

Many companies are looking for leaders who will not only volunteer themselves, but also spearhead volunteer efforts, such as an annual United Way Campaign. While being a cheerleader for a cause isn't comfortable for some introverts, being the leader who creates opportunities for others to express their passions about specific causes is a very important role. Create opportunities for others to be in the limelight, but lend your clout to the cause.

## Social Media

LinkedIn is a powerful tool to gain visibility within your industry. Invest in creating a great profile. First of all, you want a picture that is professional but reflects authenticity and approachability. Create a headline that reflects your professional brand (i.e., not just your job title), starting with a three to five word description that will show up under your headshot. For example, my headline is often something like, "The Introvert's Executive Coach." People seeing this know what I do without having to go to my full profile. Create a summary story about your job experience and achievements that points to your future aspirations. Make sure you use key words that are important in your industry so your profile shows up in searches.

Posting your own content or liking, sharing, or commenting on someone else's content not only helps you be virtually heard, but helps you to be visible to others. Use hashtags to increase your visibility to people outside of your connected network. And be diligent about expanding your LinkedIn network. While LinkedIn suggests you limit your network to those you know well, I recommend you cast your net wide, because people will begin to become familiar with you by seeing you in their content feeds.

Intentionally being visible is an important part of the mindset of a successful leader. Others look to you for leadership, but they have to be able to find you.

*I will be visible.*

# 6

# I WILL BREATHE

*Whether I am by myself or in a crowd of people, I will peri-
odically close my eyes and take deep, cleansing breaths to
re-center my thoughts and renew my energy for the task at
hand. Better yet, I will take a walk, allowing my thoughts
to wander and my mind to recharge.*

I swam on a competitive swim team when I was in high school.
Usually, at least one practice a week was focused on breathing—or,
actually, not breathing. We worked hard to build our lung capacity
to the point that the best of us could swim two lengths of freestyle
without taking a breath. When you get to that level, when your body
efficiently utilizes oxygen, you are able to focus on the race and your
stroke, not just on when you will be able to take the next breath.

During an outdoor race in the summer when I was swimming
butterfly (for non-swimmers, this is typically thought of as the most
challenging stroke), I vividly remember approaching the end of the
race, when, on an inhale, I breathed a lungful of cigar smoke thanks
to a spectator near the side of the pool. All of a sudden, my focus
shifted from finishing the race well to how I could get this pollution

out of my lungs. Rather than the expansive feeling of breathing deeply, I felt my body constrict as I struggled to finish the race.

*I will breathe*, part of *The Boldly Quiet* manifesto, is about taking care of myself. On the literal level, it means to breathe deeply during times of stress or nervousness. Metaphorically speaking, it is about mindfulness and intention, clarity of thought, and mental freedom. In this chapter, we will look at both the literal and metaphorical meanings and ways you can use breath to develop the mindset of a successful leader.

## Breathing, physiologically speaking

Have you ever been asked to give a presentation in front of a group of people you felt you needed to impress? Perhaps your boss's peers, or a large group of people who were experts on your subject matter? As you are waiting to be introduced, your palms are sweaty and your heart rate increases. You struggle to sit or stand still and you feel as though you can't remember a word of what you are about to say. These are all symptoms of the "fight or flight" response, a physiological reaction to physical or psychological danger or stress. Your body prepares to either fight the instigator of danger or flee the situation. As your breathing becomes fast and shallow, your body is not efficiently getting oxygen to your organs and your mental capacity can be negatively impacted. You may not be able to problem-solve or make decisions well when you are in "fight or flight" mode, and you may struggle to deliver a presentation or lead a meeting because you can't focus.

According to lecturer, actor, and author Brian Shapiro, author of *Exceptionally Human: Successful Communication in a Distracted World*, our breathing is generally "thoracic" —or chest breathing— where we draw the minimal amount of breath into our lungs to allow our bodily systems to function. This type of breathing is automatic and only utilizes about 10% of our lung capacity. Under stress, our chest breathing becomes even more shallow, introducing less oxygen to our systems and, ultimately, to our brain.

In contrast, diaphragmatic breathing is a more intentional method of breathing. Think of a doctor's appointment when your doctor is listening to your breathing with a stethoscope and asks you to take a deep breath. This type of breath starts by expanding the diaphragm, which creates the space for the lungs to fill with air. Deep breathing brings more oxygen to our organs and brain, which allow us to continue to function during stressful situations.[17]

Try this technique as you are reading. Inhale by first expanding your diaphragm and then breathing in for 5-10 seconds. Hold your breath for another 10-15 seconds. Then slowly exhale for 5-10 seconds. Repeat this several times. As you feel your body fill with oxygen, picture your bloodstream transporting the oxygen molecules to every part of your body. Do you feel different? Do you feel more hopeful or more alert?

From a practical perspective, you may not be able to breathe like this while you are ready to take the proverbial stage at work. But even just a few intentional deep breaths in through your nose and out through your mouth will help you stay sharp and focused.

## *Breathing, metaphorically speaking*

At the height of my career in the corporate world, I was working 50+ hours per week, providing support for my husband's consulting business, raising a child, maintaining a house and property, managing two rental properties, and facing increasing responsibility for my aging parents who lived two hours away. My mind never stopped making lists of all the things I needed to do. I struggled to relax, I struggled to stand still long enough to spend quality time with my family, and the activities I used to enjoy, like gardening, became chores. I felt I was only doing a mediocre job at everything, just trying to keep things from falling apart. I didn't have time to do anything to take care of myself, but I realized my current state of mind was not sustainable. A good friend suggested I try yoga, both for exercise and relaxation. I took her advice.

The yoga studio I joined is housed in a beautiful barn with wide-planked floors and a lofty ceiling. The large bank of windows on one side let in an abundance of natural light. As we sat on our mats at the beginning of a session, the instructor would encourage us to set our intention for our practice that day, to acknowledge our thoughts and feelings and then to put them aside without judgment, trying to quiet our minds so we could focus on our intention.

An article written by Mayo Clinic staff describes this state of mindfulness as "a type of meditation in which you focus on being intensely aware of what you're sensing and feeling in the moment, without interpretation or judgment."[18] The last part is the hardest— without interpretation or judgment. Many times when I try to acknowledge my feelings about something, I immediately become immersed in negative self-talk, which I struggle to move past. The Mayo Clinic article provides several simple ways to practice mindfulness. First, slow down and pay attention to what is around you. Use your senses. Rather than devouring your lunch because you only have five minutes between meetings, take a moment to smell and taste what you are eating. Take a walk around your building— preferably outside—and notice the sights, colors, and sounds. Stop and listen to a bird or appreciate the sight of someone being kind to another person. Again, slow down and pay attention.

Another way to practice mindfulness is to live in the moment. Instead of thinking about the next thing you need to do, focus on what you are doing right now. Really listen to what someone is saying rather than focusing on what you want to say next. Rather than skimming through the pre-reads for your next meeting, slow down, make sure you understand the material, and appreciate the work your colleague put into the topic. As you pass people in the hallway on your way to a meeting, say hello and smile. Often we are so focused on the next thing we don't even see the people we pass.

Where do you do your best thinking? For many of us, it's while taking a shower. For some, it is listening to music or exercising. For me, it's while I'm walking our German Shepherd, who is more interested in sniffing along the trail than actually exercising. Why are these types of activities conducive to clarity of thought and creativity?

Activities like these increase your body's production of dopamine, the chemical found naturally in the body that influences mood, sleep, memory, learning, concentration, and motor control.[19] Activities like these often provide an escape from the distractions that constantly plague us at work. What other things can we do to minimize

65

distractions to free our minds from clutter, giving our subconscious the space to work?

1. Take a walk. Allow your mind to wander.
2. Unplug. Many of us survived for years without internet or cell phones. Turn your devices off for at least thirty minutes every day.
3. Stop pretending that multi-tasking is efficient. It's not. Stop trying.
4. Get organized. Being surrounded by physical clutter contributes to mental clutter.
5. Create your perfect audio environment using white noise, music, or any other media that helps your frame of mind.
6. Eat well, especially fruits and vegetables high in vitamins, antioxidants, and other brain-healthy nutrients[20].

Earlier in Chapter 3, we talked about creating hope for our followers. Before we can inspire it in others, we must ourselves be hopeful in the possibility of a bright future. Without creating space to breathe, both physically and metaphorically, we will struggle to see beyond the problems and distractions in front of us. Our world will shrink and we will not experience the freedom that space brings. Picture Julie Andrews as Maria von Trapp singing "The Hills are Alive" in the movie *The Sound of Music* as she twirls in the beautiful meadow on the Austrian mountainside. When you breathe well, you feel more alive; when you mentally breathe, you do as well.

*I will breathe.*

# 7

# I WILL SURPRISE

*I will strategically and with intention sing, dance, belly-laugh, yell, or pound my fists to make people reassess their perceptions of me. I will passionately express my thoughts when I speak in front of groups, small or large, and will show my vulnerability by being able to laugh at myself.*

I was asked to give the toast at our division's year-end luncheon. Approximately 100 would be in attendance from our group, plus a group of the local sales team from another division. I wanted to do something different than the traditional, "Thank you for everything, it's been a great year" toast. What could I do to make people proud of their accomplishments for the year, happy to be at the luncheon, and looking forward to the following year? I also wanted to do something that would ensure people would hear me, as my "normal" voice tends to be on the softer side. I decided to sing the toast, replacing the words to "It's Beginning to Look a Lot Like Christmas" with references to the accomplishments of the team during the year and nods to various functional areas, designing a simple chorus that the people could easily sing with me, and ending in a grand finale. I was in a performing chorus in high school, so even though I hadn't sung in public for years, I knew I could pull it off with a little practice. My

35-minute commute the week prior was filled with me singing the spoof song over and over, building up my confidence and the strength of my voice. I must have been a sight to those in traffic around me!

On the day of the luncheon, I was nervous but determined to go through with my plan. I could barely speak to anyone, and the thought of eating any appetizers was far from my mind. What if I can't get their attention? What if I sound horrible? What if my voice cracks? Finally, everyone was seated and it was time for the show to begin. I made some reference to normally being soft-spoken, and that, in order to make sure people could hear me, I was going to sing. I will always cherish the looks on people's faces as I made that announcement and launched into my song. Eyes lit up and jaws dropped. People immediately caught onto the chorus and sang with me. Smiles and laughter filled the room and the finale was met with a standing ovation. It took me about fifteen minutes after I was done to stop shaking and to settle down enough that I could eat my lunch! And, until I left the company, people continued to comment about my performance and how fun it was.

This experience I intentionally crafted for the people attending the luncheon was successful on several different levels. First of all, the message was that the accomplishments of the team that year were recognized and appreciated. Second, even though I was one of the senior leaders in the room, I was willing to be vulnerable. And third, and perhaps most importantly, *I surprised them by doing something that seemed totally out of character for me.*

I grew up in a very musically talented family. My brother and both my sisters all played instruments in the various bands and orchestras throughout their middle and high school years. The music departments knew another sibling was coming up through the system, and I felt the weight of expectations, both from my parents and the music teachers who were eager to add another "Groves" to their roster of musicians. Like our father, my brother played the trombone, baritone, and tuba. My sisters and I played the piano—we actually had three pianos at the house at one point. My oldest sister also played the flute and piccolo, and my next oldest sister played the bassoon and various other woodwinds. I tried flute and then transitioned to French horn. Having a French horn player in the student pipeline was something the music departments were excited about. The problem was I didn't enjoy playing the French horn.

I remember sitting down with my father and talking to him about my feelings. I told him I would continue taking piano lessons, but I wanted to transition from playing an instrument to being in one of the performing choruses at school. While he wasn't necessarily happy with my decision, he supported me, even when the music teachers expressed their disappointment. I had been living in a box, the size of which determined by the expectations of those around me. I expanded the size of the box by slightly shifting people's perceptions of me. I went from "Lorraine is a talented instrumentalist, just like her siblings" to "Lorraine is a talented pianist and singer." This small shift opened up new opportunities for me.

The next, more radical shift, came when I joined the swim team. My family was full of musicians. We enjoyed athletics, but weren't necessarily athletes. The "last Groves" was shaking things up! I was far from the best swimmer on the team, but I enjoyed the challenge. I also enjoyed the sense of freedom that came with my box becoming even bigger. I experienced new opportunities and relationships because I pushed the limits of people's perceptions of me. I went from "Lorraine is a talented pianist and singer" to "Lorraine is a talented pianist and singer—and she swims butterfly and breaststroke!"

How does this apply in the business world? I believe if you don't periodically push the boundaries of people's perceptions of you, the walls of your leadership box will become more and more restrictive. The point where it is impossible to step outside of the boundaries *because we start believing the boundaries drawn by people's perceptions of us are real.* And, if your primary label for yourself is "introvert," people's perceptions of you, i.e., the box, will be shaped by that stereotype.

What is the stereotypical view of an introvert? Someone who is quiet, often thought of as shy, prefers to be alone, avoids conflict, doesn't seek or desire attention, thinks deeply, prefers to write, listens intently, and is definitely not assertive. Since many of these stereotypical traits are the antithesis of the stereotype of a successful leader, the leader labeled as an introvert is automatically at a disadvantage, beginning with a handicap in the competition for new opportunities. In her book *Rebel Talent: Why it Pays to Break the Rules at Work and in Life,* Francesco Gino, a well-respected author, researcher, and professor at Harvard Business School, tells us:

> *"Stereotypes can help us make sense of the world. But because they are mere generalizations, they can also stir up a great deal of trouble . . . When we buy into stereotypes, we can sometimes end up perpetrators of cruelty and discrimination, often without even being aware of it . . . When we're not careful, stereotypes act like firewalls, blocking new information from*

*penetrating our thoughts and preventing us from changing our*
*minds unless something truly dramatic happens.*"[21]

A softer phrase to describe this phenomenon is "accidental diminisher," where, because we think we equate who someone is or how they think with a stereotype, we often say stupid and insensitive things that reinforce the negative aspects of the stereotype. I was at a networking event and the head of the organization, an HR executive, asked me how I could handle the business development aspect of being self-employed since I was an introvert. While it may have seemed to this person like a logical and appropriate question, the implied message was that introverts cannot be successful as independent consultants. I left the meeting angry with him, but also with a seed of self-doubt. What if he was right?

What about the well-meaning, self-appointed leader of a discussion who, in line with the training she has received about leading small groups, says during a pause in a robust discussion, "Let's give our quiet members a chance to speak," implying we introverts are not capable of inserting ourselves into conversations when we have something to say. If I don't come up with something to say—even if I have nothing to add to the conversation—the walls of the box surrounding me become stronger and more restrictive.

Gino discusses the concept of "stereotype threat," or the tendency to "choke" and underperform due to the fear of bias. If I am reminded I am an introvert at the beginning of a meeting, I am more apt to act like the stereotypical introvert during the meeting. If, conversely, I am reminded I am a successful leader at the beginning of a meeting, my performance during the meeting will be more confident and engaged. According to Gino:

71

"The consequences of stereotype [can cause us to] find ourselves closed off from others, less ambitious, and disengaged from our work, unable to fulfill our potential as leaders, negotiators, entrepreneurs, and competitors. Of course, the consequences hurt not only those who experience the threat, but also their organizations. And a vicious cycle develops: When women experience stereotype threat, their mental energy is taxed as they work to disprove the stereotype, leaving them with less mental energy to perform the task at hand. This creates more stress and lower performance— thus maintaining the under-representation of women in the workplace, especially in leadership positions. All of us are part of some group that can be affected by negative perceptions, and we know we may be judged by it.[22]

Gino then encourages us to rebel against the stereotypes that limit our confidence and, ultimately, our performance. To continue my box metaphor, rebelling against the stereotype that constrains us means to intentionally and strategically expand the walls of your box. How? By doing something "truly dramatic" that chips away, if not totally shatters, the stereotype that encases you. And you don't have to work too hard to do the truly dramatic. Ask yourself these questions to get started:

*What hidden talents or skills do you have? What do you like to do for fun?*

My hidden talent at work was my musical ability. I also am an avid gardener and enjoy baking (my grandmother passed down a wonderful banana bread recipe!). In addition to singing a toast at the holiday lunch, I stretched the boundaries of my box by volunteering with other (mainly non-executive) associates at a community garden. I was also known to talk to people about perennials and bring in day lilies and other diggings from my garden. Loaves of banana bread would mysteriously show up in the kitchen for all to share. Take something you already do and bring it to work so people can see you in a different light.

*When you make people laugh, what are you doing or saying? What makes you laugh?*

I love puns. And I will laugh (or at least groan) every time I hear one, even if I have heard it many times before. I allow myself to laugh out loud and enjoy the moment publicly. Laughter is contagious. Help people around you laugh. Sometimes when I think of a good pun, the moment has passed. If I can't redirect the conversation, I tuck it away so I am ready the next time the opportunity arises. I'm not very good at telling jokes, but enjoy the people who are. Allow yourself to laugh out loud. Loudly.

*What situations cause you to naturally assert yourself?*

During a master's course I took at the University of Pennsylvania, Dr. Rod Napier, an esteemed professor, consultant, and author, led the class through a self-awareness/team dynamics exercise which included a short self-assessment and group discussion. When I volunteered to have him openly discuss his insights about my assessment, he fondly told me that under stress, and particularly when I feel someone is being taken advantage of, I can be a "brick shithouse on wheels." I had never been called that before, but as we discussed what he meant, I realized Dr. Napier was absolutely right. In fact, when I called my husband on my way home from class and told him what

Dr. Napier said, he laughed and said, "That's a good description of you sometimes!"

How can I use this to surprise others? While I tend to express myself in softer tones, I find people look at me differently when I allow myself to have a controlled blow-up. Granted, I have had this approach backfire a few times. But when the people in the room with me need an advocate, I naturally become. When I turn my volume up a notch people notice, and the box of people's perceptions of me gets a little larger.

*I will surprise. Your box is too small for me.*

# 8

# I WILL GROW

*I will surround myself with diversity so I can understand different perspectives and make better decisions. I will celebrate failures, seeing in them an opportunity to learn, and will surround myself with people who challenge me by being better than I am in areas and who will provide me with authentic feedback. I will intentionally expose myself to new ideas.*

I graduated from the College of William & Mary in the spring of 1985 at the age of twenty. I struggled quite a bit my sophomore year, failing two classes as I worked through lack of direction, poor study skills, and distracting family issues. I was lucky to graduate in four years, and I never looked back. I prided myself on being an "on-the-job learner" and felt a master's degree would not help me or my career. In fact, most of the MBA graduates I hired seemed to know a lot, except the one thing that was important to me—how to actually do a job!

Fast forward to the summer of 2013. I had just successfully orchestrated a two-phase organizational change and found I loved the project. I was able to take a very complex situation and break it down into pieces and then rebuild it into something that at least had a shot at being more effective than the current structure. I worked with the impacted teams and their leaders and partnered with human resources to roll out the changes. At a one-to-one meeting with my boss after the conclusion of the project, he suggested I look into the University of Pennsylvania's Organizational Dynamics Master's Program. My initial reaction was to laugh. I didn't like school. Plus, I was 48 years old. How could school help me at this point in my life?

Since my boss was the one who had made the suggestion, I decided it would be a good idea to attend an informational meeting on the program, just so I could say I did. Larry Starr, the chair of the department, made a compelling case for the program, and I decided to apply. I became a little worried when I had to get my transcript from William & Mary—I had never even found out what my final grade point average was! I wrote two great essays and thought that, along with my work experience, my acceptance was a slam dunk. When I received word I could take up to two classes as a probationary student and had to prove I could achieve a certain grade in both classes before I would be formally accepted into the program, I got a little mad. Well, a lot mad. Remember the "brick shithouse on wheels?" I briefly went down the path of "if they don't want me, their loss" and quickly landed on "I will show them!" I signed up for my first class, Systems and Design Thinking, and was totally blown away. I remember driving home from class the first night, mind spinning, wide awake, ready to solve all the problems at work the next day!

As I progressed through the program, I interacted with so many people—both professors and students—who had life experiences so different from mine. International students who were often quiet

76

because English was their second language, but who had marvelous perspectives on topics. Academicians challenged our thinking processes and pushed us to go deep into topics that were (generally) interesting and relevant to our day-to-day professional lives. Students currently working across a spectrum of organizations—private, public, non-profit, academic—and across industries. We talked in Chapter 3 about embracing the perspectives of others so they feel heard and respected. It is also important to seek out perspectives other than your own so you can grow.

## Pursuing Growth

Reading a book like this is one way you can pursue growth. Stretching your brain muscles, thinking about something new, putting yourself in new situations, taking risks, pushing the box you find yourself in to new limits: these are all ways to pursue growth. How can you pursue growth within the context of your work environment? First of all, talk to your boss. Leaders who understand the value of retention, engagement, and results support creating development opportunities for their high performers, especially those who show they are interested in growing and learning. Your human resources partner is also a good source for learning about and taking advantage of development resources within your organization. These resources could include webinars, group workshops, mentoring, and coaching, or even third-party programs like executive education through a local university or external organizations. These are usually less than a week long and can provide valuable tools for growth.

What if you work for a smaller organization that doesn't have the infrastructure in place to formally develop its talented employees? Here are a few options:

*Pursue an advanced degree:* Many academic institutions have night classes or online programs available for students who are also working full-time. And many companies offer some type of tuition reimbursement for classwork that is relevant to your role. But, if that's not an issue, perhaps you can focus on an area you've always been interested in but thought it was too late to explore.

*Attend Industry networking groups and conferences:* Many industry groups offer great content and resources. Not only will you be mingling with others interested in the same topics as you are, keynote and breakout session speakers often bring insights and different perspectives to the topics at hand.

*Private coaching:* Most leadership coaches have two types of packages: one set offered directly to individuals, the other offered to corporations. Do your homework before you hire a private coach. Make sure a coaching package is set up to meet your specific needs by thinking through what you want to accomplish through coaching and how you want the coach to work with you. And when you do your initial consultation with your coach, you want to walk away with an idea of whether your coach is a good fit and if he or she will be able to help you achieve your goals.

*Reading/Podcasts:* Several years ago, my husband bought me a Kindle for my birthday, and I thought I wouldn't like it. To my surprise, I loved not having to lug around books, to the point where I now just read my fiction books through an app on my cell phone.

I have found, however, I still need physical books for my non-fiction reading so I can mark pages, highlight sections, and write in the margins, making the content I found meaningful easily retrievable. Regardless, you can consume content in many ways today. Look for good content from reputable sources. And I encourage you to look at _their_ sources—the references listed in the back of a good book can be a treasure trove of additional learning.

## _Experiential Growth_

I ran across a graphic on LinkedIn a long time ago that I printed out and kept because it was a good reminder about framing our thoughts in a way that encourages growth, not dissatisfaction. The words "growth mindset" are written on a hand-drawn picture of a brain, and around the brain were negative words that were crossed out and replaced with positive alternatives. The following table helps illustrate the shift in mindset if you look at the challenging situations through a growth lens.

| Negative Mindset | Growth Mindset |
|---|---|
| I can't believe I ran into this roadblock on my project. Now I'm going to miss my deadline and look bad to my boss. | This roadblock may make me miss my deadline, but I can see an opportunity to show my team how a leader successfully addresses this situation. |
| My co-worker has been getting a lot of attention because of the presentation she gave. I bet I could have done a better job than she did. | My co-worker did a great job on her presentation. I should congratulate her and maybe get some tips. |
| I gave some tough feedback today to one of my team members. He became very defensive and it was a horrible discussion. I hate being a manager. | I gave some tough feedback to one of my team members. It didn't go very well. I wonder how I could have approached the discussion differently? |

| Negative Mindset | Growth Mindset |
|---|---|
| My team members keep asking me how they can help me, but I don't like to delegate. It's too hard to teach everybody what to do and I will probably do a better job myself! | Delegation can be hard when I can probably do a better job myself, but investing in my people so they can eventually learn how to do these tasks on their own is worth my time and effort. |
| My boss returned my PowerPoint draft and it was all marked up. I feel like such a failure. She probably thought everything I wrote was garbage. | My boss returned my PowerPoint draft and it was all marked up. She gave me great feedback that will help me prepare something that is very insightful and valuable to my audience. |
| How am I supposed to know the answer to that question? | Hmm. Interesting question. Let me do some research and find out! |

My son, Tyler, is my hero when it comes to intentionally seeking growth opportunities. As I write this, he is preparing to go to France for his junior year of high school. He told us during his freshman year that this is something he wanted to do. My husband and I said we would support him in doing this, but he had to do the research (we sort of thought he would decide it was too much effort and then move on!). Tyler pushed forward in his quest and gathered information from guidance counselors, teachers, and an exchange student currently at his school. He reached out to the local Rotary Club and an organization called Youth for Understanding. He arrived at the point where he couldn't go any further on his own and engaged us in the process. As the logistics have fallen into place, he has worked hard on his language skills, both through school and at home. He is excited about the unknown — and probably a little nervous — because this experience represents just the starting point of his journey to be culturally and linguistically fluent in many languages and countries. Talk about a growth mindset!

Consider a sponge. As you add water, the sponge expands until it reaches its full potential. As it dries, the sponge contracts, sometimes even smaller than its original state. We are like that sponge. We must find a catalyst to help us reach our potential. And if we don't keep pursuing our potential through intentional growth, our world view becomes smaller and smaller.

Intentional growth takes courage.

*I will grow.*

# Conclusion

One professor I had during my undergraduate studies at William & Mary stands out in my memory. On the last day of class, Thomas Finn, emeritus chancellor professor of religion, masterfully took the content of the semester to a deeper, more meaningful level. His conclusion brought in strands of concepts from his introduction on the first day of class all the way through to the last class and wove them together as only great orators can. I literally remember smiling as I walked out of class because his conclusion was so powerful.

As I approached writing the last chapter of this book, I thought of this professor and whether I could come close to achieving what he did during that class in a small room in Williamsburg, Virginia. And I realized for this book to be true to my vision, the job of writing the perfect conclusion belongs to the reader, perhaps prompted by the questions below. I realize many of you will probably just skim the questions. I encourage you, however, to invest the time in yourself and your own development by going back, reflecting on, and writing down responses. I guarantee you will be on the right track to changing how others perceive you if you work through the questions and answer them thoughtfully.

*Questions for Reflection*

1. Why were you interested in reading this book? What problem were you trying to solve? Where are your pain points?
2. Of the seven items in *The Boldly Quiet Manifesto*, which one(s) resonated the most with you? Where you felt if you thought about yourself differently you would make the most progress in your leadership journey? [The seven items are: I will embrace myself, I will embrace others, I will be heard, I will be visible, I will breathe, I will surprise, I will grow.]
3. For each one that you selected in #2, complete the following sentences, avoiding the words "not," "but," and "except."

   - I am in the process of learning to [the *Manifesto* point].
   - I love the idea of _____
     _____.
   - It makes me happy to see the potential I have to _____
     _____.
   - I am excited to think I can replace the sometimes negative label of "introvert" and take on the positive, fulfilling label(s) of "_____
     _____."

For example, this is my current answer to #3:

*I am in the process of learning to embrace myself. I love the idea of believing I have unique strengths that make me uniquely qualified to be exactly what certain clients look for in a coach. It makes me happy to see the potential I have to make an incredibly positive impact on other people's lives and careers. I am excited to think I can replace the sometimes-negative label of "introvert" and take on the positive, fulfilling label of "successful author, speaker, and coach."*

I was led through a similar exercise by a fellow Strengths coach, Rhonda Knight Boyle, on a group coaching call. Rhonda was so bold as to promise the group that each of us would see an opportunity within 24 hours that we probably wouldn't have noticed before. Why? Because our mindset was different. We would be looking up and out, not down and in. We would be focused on potential, not limits. I encourage you to reset your mindset so you are focused on your potential, not your perception of your limits. Hopefully this book has given you some tools and a new pair of glasses through which to view yourself. Being an introvert is an important piece of who you are, but there are many more aspects I encourage you to explore.

I am in the process of becoming a successful leader because:

- I embrace who I am so I can be authentic and confident.
- I embrace others so I can help them achieve their potential.
- I am heard because I have valuable things to say.
- I am visible because I am engaged.
- I breathe so I will be energized and full of life.
- I surprise so no one will take me for granted.
- I grow because the journey never stops.

# AUTHOR REFERENCES AND NOTES

1 Jacquelyn Strickland is a Licensed Professional Counselor, Coach and workshop leader based in Fort Collins, Colorado. She has been a certified trainer in the Myers-Briggs Personality Inventory since 1991. Her counseling and coaching practice specializes in blending therapeutic principles and coaching strategies with a spiritual foundation. She and Dr. Elaine Aron are co-founders of the HSP Gathering Retreats™. More information can be found at http://www.lifeworkshelp.com/

2 Susan Cain, *Quiet: The Power of Introverts in a World That Can't Stop Talking* (New York: Broadway Books, 2012), 269.

3 Jacquelyn Strickland, "Introversion, Extroversion and the Highly Sensitive Person," April 24, 2018, https://hsperson.com/introversion-extroversion-and-the-highly-sensitive-person/

4 Elena Lytkina Botelho, et al. "What Sets Successful CEOs Apart." *Harvard Business Review*. May-June 2017.

5 Amy Cuddy. *Presence: Bringing Your Boldest Self to Your Biggest Challenges*, (New York, Little, Brown Stark, 2015), 89.

6 Cindy Schwartz-Devol, Ph.D. has been a licensed Psychologist since 2002, supporting others on their journeys to be healthier and more integrated, to enjoy relationships with themselves and others. Cindy treasures all of her eclectic training and, in accordance with her own background and interests, Cindy has developed a niche in working with highly sensitive people and athletes. More information can be found at http://www.cindyschwartz-devolphd.com/

7 Russell Ackoff. *Re-Creating the Corporation: A Design of Organizations for the 21st Century*, (New York, Oxford University Press, Inc., 1999), 13-14. Ackoff gives a simple example of the difference between *solution* and *dissolution*: paper matchbooks originally had the striking area (i.e., the abrasive strip) on

the front of the matchbook, so if you opened the matchbook, took and lit a match, a spark could potentially light the rest of the matches on fire due to the striking area's proximity to the rest of the matches. A way to try to *solve* this issue was to place the words, "Close Cover Before Striking" on the front of the matchbook cover to warn the match strikers to protect themselves against burnt fingers. *The way to dissolve this issue was to move the striking area to the back of the matchbook, away from the rest of the matches.* The problem disappeared.

8 Jo Self is a Gallup-Certified Strengths Coach who offers master classes, team workshops, and individual coaching in both English and Spanish. The master class I attended was called Strengths, Unleashed: Unleash your confidence, unleash your voice, and unleash your brand. Jo can be contacted through her website at https://joself.consulting/.

9 Tom Rath and Barry Conchie. *Strengths-based Leadership* (New York, Gallup Press, 2008), 80-91.

10 "Johari Window," Business Jargons, accessed July 30, 2019, www.businessjargons.com/johari-window.html

11 Donald O. Clifton and Paula Nelson. *Soar with your Strengths* (New York, Random House Publishing Group, 1992), 20.

12 James Kouzes and Barry Posner. *The Leadership Challenge: How to Make Extraordinary Things Happy in Organizations* (5th ed.) (The Leadership Challenge®, a Wiley Brand, 2012). 68.

13 Bob Kantor. *Shatter Your Leadership Limits: Better Results in Less Time with Less Stress* (United States, Motivational Press, 2012). 57.

14 Jennifer B. Kahnweiler. The Introverted Leader: Building on Your Quiet Strength (2nd ed.). (Oakland, CA, Berrett-Koehler Publishers, Inc., 2018). 15-16.

15 Jan Stefanski is the owner of Janus Consulting, a consulting firm in the greater Philadelphia area. Jan helps individual employees, groups, and organizations achieve sustainable business success through strategy sessions, implementation planning, skills development and coaching. Jan can be contacted through his website at www.janusconsulting.com.

16 Erin Owen, MBA, PCC, JCTC, draws on nearly 25 years of professional experience ranging from organizational change management consulting to leadership coaching, in which she has consulted with and coached hundreds of entrepreneurs, business leaders and private individuals from more than 15

countries in the Americas, Europe, and Asia. Erin can be contacted through her website, https://erinowen.com/

17 Brian Shapiro. *Exceptionally Human: Successful Communication in a Distracted World* (Philadelphia, PA, Shapiro Communications Publishing, 2016), p. 127-130.

18 "Mindfulness Exercises: See How Mindfulness Helps You Live in the Moment," Mayo Clinic, accessed June 8, 2019, https://www.mayoclinic.org/healthy-lifestyle/consumer-health/in-depth/mindfulness-exercises/art-20046356

19 Bethany Cadman and Suzanne Falck (reviewer), "Dopamine Deficiency: What You Need to Know," Medical News Today, accessed June 10, 2019, last reviewed January 17, 2018. https://www.medicalnewstoday.com/articles/320637.php

20 "How to Improve Concentration and Mental Clarity," Shift, accessed June 10, 2019, https://www.shift.is/2015/03/how-to-improve-concentration-and-mental-clarity/

21 Francesca Gino. Rebel Talent: Why it Pays to Break the Rules at Work and in Life (New York, Dey Books, 2018), 113.

22 Gino, *Rebel Talent*, 123-124

# BIBLIOGRAPHY

Ackoff, Russell. *Re-Creating the Corporation: A Design of Organizations for the 21st Century.* New York: Oxford University Press, Inc., 1999.

Botelho, E. L., Powell, K. R., Kincaid, S. and Wang, D. "What Sets Successful CEOs Apart." *Harvard Business Review.* May-June 2017.

Business Jargons. "Johari Window." Accessed July 30, 2019, www.businessjargons.com/johari-window.html

Cadman, Bethany and Falck, Suzanne (reviewer), "Dopamine Deficiency: What You Need to Know," Medical News Today. Accessed June 10, 2019, last reviewed January 17, 2018. https://www.medicalnewstoday.com/articles/320637.php

Cain, Susan, *Quiet: The Power of Introverts in a World That Can't Stop Talking.* New York: Broadway Books, 2012.

Clifton, Donald O. and Nelson, Paula. *Soar with your Strengths.* New York, Random House Publishing Group, 1992.

Cuddy, Amy. *Presence: Bringing Your Boldest Self to Your Biggest Challenges.* New York, Little, Brown Stark, 2015.

Gino, Francesca. *Rebel Talent: Why it Pays to Break the Rules at Work and in Life* New York, Dey Books, 2018.

Kahnweiler, Jennifer B. *The Introverted Leader: Building on Your Quiet Strength* (2nd ed.). (Oakland, CA, Berrett-Koehler Publishers, Inc., 2018).

Kantor, Bob. *Shatter Your Leadership Limits: Better Results in Less Time with Less Stress*. United States, Motivational Press, 2012.

Kouzes, James and Posner, Barry. *The Leadership Challenge: How to Make Extraordinary Things Happy in Organizations* (5th ed.). The Leadership Challenge®, a Wiley Brand, 2012.

Mayo Clinic. "Mindfulness Exercises: See How Mindfulness Helps You Live in the Moment," https://www.mayoclinic.org/healthy-lifestyle/consumer-health/in-depth/mindfulness-exercises/art-20046356

Rath, Tom and Conchie, Barry. *Strengths-based Leadership*. New York: Gallup Press, 2008.

Shapiro, Brian. *Exceptionally Human: Successful Communication in a Distracted World*. Philadelphia, PA, Shapiro Communications Publishing, 2016.

Shift. "How to Improve Concentration and Mental Clarity." Accessed June 10, 2019, https://www.shift.is/2015/03/how-to-improve-concentration-and-mental-clarity/

Strickland, Jacquelyn. "Introversion, Extroversion and the Highly Sensitive Person," April 24, 2018, https://hsperson.com/introversion-extroversion-and-the-highly-sensitive-person/

# About the Author

Lorraine McCamley is the owner of Boldly Quiet Consulting. She spent years in the corporate world feeling that being an introvert was something to be ashamed of or fixed. She now coaches quiet professionals, helping them understand and embrace who they are so they can authentically and effectively lead others and prepare for that next step in their career journey. Lorraine is a Gallup-Certified Strengths Coach and holds a master's degree in organizational dynamics from the University of Pennsylvania. She is an avid reader of crime fiction and can often be found tending her garden.